MW00680551

WHAT A COMPUT- ER CAN DO FOR YOU

irv brechner

illustrated at
blue egg studios

Published By WIDL Video, Chicago IL, 60639

©1983, IRV BRECHNER

All rights reserved. No part of this book may be reproduced or transmitted in any form or by any means, electronic, mechanical, or chemical, including photocopying, recording, or by any information storage and/or retrieval system, without prior permission in writing from the publisher.

WIDL VIDEO, Chicago
5245 W. Diversey Ave.
Chicago, Illinois 60639
[312]-622-9606

Printed In The United States of America

INTRODUCTION

Millions of personal computers have already been sold in a few short years. They are popping up everywhere—in business, doctor's offices and in homes.

Recently, Time Magazine's man of the year was not a man or woman...but a machine, the computer.

With all this activity, publicity, promotion and hulabaloo going on, it seems as if predictions of a computer in every home might eventually happen.

But one question keeps coming up, over and over again, in all my conversations with people: What can I do with a personal computer?

The commonly touted uses of a computer—word processing, data base management and financial analysis are words which I never understood before getting into computers, and words which probably mean little or nothing to a vast majority of the population.

This unawareness of the large number of potential uses for a personal computer is the reason for this book. You will not find, in this book, programs which you can put right into your Apple or Atari home computer. You will not find instructions on using your TRS-80 or IBM personal computer. Nor will you find software evaluations of programs for your Texas Instruments or Pet computer.

Instead, you will find ideas by the dozens. Different, imaginative ways in which you can use your computer. You'll learn about programming and buying software once you get into computers, but first it is necessary that you can answer our question: "What can I do with a personal computer?"

The answer to that question takes the shape of five distinct areas: home uses, small business uses, educational uses, entertainment and communications. Thirty two areas are examined in those five categories, and suggestions for use within each area are presented.

While you won't be able to actually program a computer or find the correct software from this book, you will, after reading it, be able to answer our question. You'll know how you'll intend to use your personal computer; you'll know what can be done with one. And when people ask you what you can do with your personal computer, you'll be able to explain word processing, data base management and much more!

Table of Contents

Introduction

Home Uses for A Personal Computer

Business Uses For A Personal Computer

Education Uses For A Personal Computer

Entertainment With A Personal Computer

Communicating With A Personal Computer

WHAT A COMPUTER CAN DO FOR YOU

Home Uses For A Personal Computer

Data Base Management System

DATA BASE MANAGEMENT SYSTEM

The Heart of Most Computer Applications

Yes, it does sound like a mouthful, that you'd prefer to ignore, but understanding DBMS is probably the single most important concept to spend time with.

All of the ideas presented here, and most commercial programs rely on some form of data base management, so understanding it is critical.

In order to make DBMS meaningful, let's split it up into three parts: Data, Base, and Management System. We'll look at each one separately and then the combination of the three will become obvious.

DATA

Quite simply, DATA is information. Data comes in many different forms—a list of customers in a store, sales by month for a business, a list of a company's employees, etc. Anything there is can be classified as data—the houses on your block, the shirts you own, or the cans of soup in your food closet.

Data in its raw form, just sitting there, is really useless. But when you have the ability to collect and manipulate it, it becomes meaningful.

BASE

For our purposes, a BASE is a collection...of, you guessed it, data. Therefore, a data base is nothing more than an orderly collection of data which can be managed to produce results which help an individual or business. Your telephone book is a data base. So are your income tax records.

What makes a data base useful is the ability to perform certain functions upon it—sorting, producing reports and mailing labels, adding numbers, searching for certain items, etc.

MANAGEMENT SYSTEM

In the broadest sense, a MANAGEMENT SYSTEM is a method by which one can manage or control something. A baseball manager's ability to control his team is a management system; so is the telephone company's capability to complete millions of phone calls at one time.

When a management system is used to manage a data base, we come to the management of information. The heart of computing.

Putting it all together, we see that a data base can be managed by a special system to produce meaningful information which can be used in any way to benefit the end user!

So all four words together - DATA BASE MANAGEMENT SYSTEM - constitute a powerful concept which is the cornerstone of computing on all levels, from the smallest personal microcomputer to the largest giant mainframe.

The computer, through a DBMS, manages information. Whether it be a holiday shopping list of a few dozen people, or charge accounts of millions of customers, the concept is still the same: a data base of information managed by a special system to produce meaningful information.

HOW A DBMS IS ORGANIZED

Learning the simple principles behind the organization and use of a DBMS will show you why they are so widely used and effective.

Let's start with your objectives, which generally are to take a bunch of information, organize it and draw useable information from it. Suppose you are president of a computer club having 100 members.

Each member fills out a card upon joining, which contains: name, address, city, state, zip, phone. In addition to this basic information you also have amount of membership dues paid, type of computer the person owns, computing languages he programs in, and so forth. Let's look at the ways this information can be used if set up properly in a DBMS.

(1) You could get mailing labels to each member whenever you sent out your club newsletter.

(2) You could get a phone list with members' name and phone number should you wish to call them.

(3) You could see who has paid up his membership, and add the total amount of dues received.

(4) If you wanted to do a special product involving the Persimmon Computer, you could sort out only those members who have one.

(5) If you were invited to give a talk on the Pascal programming

language, you could search for those members who know Pascal. (6) You could combine any of the above to save you time and money!

The point here is simple: we set up the DBMS based upon what information we want to get out of it later on. We put in as much information as necessary to get the results desired.

For our example, let's say we wanted all of the above computer club information to be set up in a DBMS. Before we continue, a word about commercially available DBMS is important. You can buy many different DBMS software programs. While each will differ in several areas, most have the capabilities we will explore in our example.

The first step is to define the parameters of the file, which we would call COMPUTER CLUB MEMBERSHIP FILE. You will be asked for the number of fields you desire. A field is an item of information. One field is the members name, another is the address, and so on. You will also be asked for the length of each field, or the number of characters long.

The longer the fields, the fewer number of records the diskette can hold. You'll learn to make field lengths as short as possible where desirable.

Using our example, a complete list of the fields, numbered 1 through 9, with each field length in parentheses:

1. MEMBER NAME (25)
2. ADDRESS (30)
3. CITY (30)
4. STATE (02)
5. ZIP (05)
6. PHONE (12)
7. DUES PAID (10)
8. COMPUTER (10)
9. LANGUAGE (10)

By adding up the lengths of each field, the maximum length of the entire record is 134 characters. But for insurance, let's add another blank field, #10, labeled MISCELLANEOUS and with a length of 15. This is because we may want to, at a later date, add new information.

At this point, when you indicate all is correct, the computer will set up this information, so that whenever you use this file, all the data will be in this format you just entered. Because it isn't always easy to change the format, you should take great care to think of all the alternatives you might want before completing this start-up section.

At this particular point, you will be most likely returned to the main menu, which will list all the options open to you. Each option (and there are additional ones that vary from program to program) will be explained below; knowing all your options will give you the ability to properly define your initial fields as just presented.

ENTER DATA

Here you are usually shown the number of records (members, in our case) already on file, with the computer prompting you to enter new information field by field. First you'd be asked for members name, then address, then city, and so on. You can skip a field and then later fill it in.

CHANGE DATA

Here you have the ability to go into your file of members, and change any field(s) you wish. Suppose someone moves, and you want to put in the new address...Simple. You do it, field by field for that members' record.

DELETE DATA

This option gives you the ability to delete one or more records. When someone drops out of the group, you'll probably want to delete his record...Easy with this option.

LIST DATA

This routine enables you to print out information in many different ways. Two common examples are mailing labels and reports. You will be asked which fields you want to print and in which order. You can print them horizontally across a sheet of paper or vertically on a label. You don't have to print all the fields. Fancier programs have all kinds of exciting ways to create reports and listings.

6

SORT DATA

Here you can take your records and sort them in most any fashion. You can alphabetize your club list, for example. Other possible sorts outside of our example include by date, number amounts, zip codes, etc. The sort option is an incredible time saver—think of how much hand work is involved to alphabetize 550 names—a lot more than the couple of minutes it takes with the computer.

SEARCH DATA

This is similar to sort, but without rearranging the order of the data. Here you might ask for all the members names who own a Persimmon computer, and that's all you get. If you wanted Persimmon owners PLUS those who know Pascal, you'll get just that group. Programs offer you the ability to search many fields at the same time—I think you can see the advantages here!

MATH OPTION

Here you can perform arithmetic functions, including totaling, averaging, etc., on numbers found in any field. In our example, you could add up the total membership dues found in field #7.

INDEX DATA

With this option, you can create an index like you might find in the back of a book. In our example, you could index members by name!

OTHER OPTIONS

There are many others including COMPARE DATA (compare data in different records but in the same field), REPLACE DATA (replace large blocks of data), FILE INFORMATION (see how many records you have and the space that is used), PRINTER SET UP (what printer variables - spacing, line length, etc.) are available, and so forth. The basic options have been explained; the others you will become acquainted with when you buy a specific program.

At this point, the uses for a DBMS should be crystal clear. If not, please re-read this section. You must have a clear understanding of this concept to grasp the full computing power presented in the balance of this book. In fact, examples in each section will refer back to the options given in this chapter, so please make sure they're clear.

What should emerge besides an understanding of how the DBMS concept works is that you can manipulate, use and process the same information in many different ways. This multiple processing of your data is the key to Data Base Management Systems. Make sure you know it well!

WHAT A COMPUTER CAN DO FOR YOU

Home Uses For A Personal Computer

Family Record Management

FAMILY RECORD MANAGEMENT

Most families keep their important papers in one or more of the following places: safe deposit box, old shoeboxes, file drawers, a wall safe, under the mattress, and so forth. While we can discuss all day the merits of each, the computer can make organization of your family records a snap. Personal papers include insurance policies, medical records, stock and financial investment certificates, report cards, credit card numbers, etc. All of these items, plus many others you can think of, should be stored on a computer diskette, with one backup kept in a fireproof place.

As with most every idea in this book, a data base can be set up to handle FAMILY RECORD MANAGEMENT. You might want to set up 11 fields in this area to store the following information:

1 NAME OF COMPANY
2 DATE
3 ADDRESS
4 CITY/STATE/ZIP
5 PHONE
6 REPRESENTATIVE
7 SERIAL NUMBER
8 EXPIRATION DATE
9 VALUE/COST
10 COMMENTS
11 MISC

As you can see, these fields will hold information for most any family record, plus the 11th field, a miscellaneous one, can be used for additional information. Most of the fields will be up to 30 characters long, but 'comments' can be much longer.

From this arrangement, you can list all your records by company, print out a phone list, or keep track of records by date initiated or expiration date, whichever is appropriate.

Keeping accurate track of family records is important, especially for insurance purposes. But when you need information in a hurry and don't have time to search, the information is at your fingertips. It is, as with most every case, worth the extra work in the beginning to set it all up.

WHAT A COMPUTER CAN DO FOR YOU

Home Uses For A Personal Computer

Area
3

List Management

LIST MANAGEMENT

If you were to think about how many different groups of items around your home that could be classified into lists, you'd be amazed. For this reason, you might consider using a DBMS to organize the following classes of information:

- master gift list
- address and phone list
- phonograph record/tape list
- book list
- magazine subscription list

Now the first question you'll probably ask is 'why keep a list of books'? Being an author, I have all my books on a DBMS classified by subject for research purposes. Obviously, not everyone would benefit from a book list, but it is a viable example for many people, who might want to reference books or magazine articles for their jobs.

One good example is your master gift list, which can be sorted or searched by type of ocassion (holiday season), month (to get upcoming birthdays) or by name of person involved.

As with family records, LIST MANAGEMENT should be approached the same way. Set up your fields to yield the information you need at the end. For example, let's look at the magazine subscription list. How many times have you wondered about your renewal status? If you've moved, then you know the long time it takes to track down all your subscription address change forms. Here's a better way—set up the magazine subscription list on your computer with the following fields:

1 NAME OF PUBLICATION
2 ADDRESS
3 CITY/STATE ZIP
4 TELEPHONE
5 LENGTH OF SUBSCRIPTION
6 PRICE
7 EXPIRATION DATE
8 ORDERED BY WHOM
9 MISCELLANEOUS

If you want a complete list of all subscriptions and what they are costing you per year (for tax purposes!), you can get it. If you are moving, you can print a 'change of address notification' and send it to every publication on the list. If you didn't get an issue or two, you have the address and phone number at your disposal. Well organized and productive people all make lists. It keeps their flow of information organized. The same is true in a well run household. Consider making lists like the ones above, plus many others you can dream up!

WHAT A COMPUTER CAN DO FOR YOU

Home Uses For A Personal Computer

Area
4

Financial Management

FINANCIAL MANAGEMENT

The use of your personal computer to keep track of family financial affairs is the application that comes to mind most often. While it is very important, we should keep in mind that it is still just one of many uses.

FINANCIAL MANAGEMENT includes the balancing of your checkbooks—most families have more than one—so that time consuming reconciliations are permanently stored on the diskette. The speed of the computations is increased, and the likelihood of an addition or subtraction error is basically nonexistent. Another use in this area is figuring mortgage payments. With the many different types of mortgages now available, you must make every dollar count. With programs especially designed for this purpose, you can look at all the alternatives open to you, compare them, and choose the best one.

Another area which most people have some trouble with is the computation of interest. Whether it be on a savings account, car loan, second mortgage or any other situation where you're borrowing money, knowing the monthly payments as well as the total cost might give you a better perspective. For example, would you buy that new car if you knew the total cost, including interest on the loan was $13,500 for an $8,000 car? Perhaps yes, perhaps not, but you now have the ability to add new information to your decision making process.

These programs usually give you a menu offering the different types of computations available, into which you must plug the appropriate numbers: amount of loan, interest rate, length of period, etc.

This is one of the few programs that really isn't a database. Some of the more advanced programs will let you store data on different alternatives or take the same data and analyze it in several different ways.

WHAT A COMPUTER CAN DO FOR YOU

Home Uses For A Personal Computer

Area
5

Family Budget Management

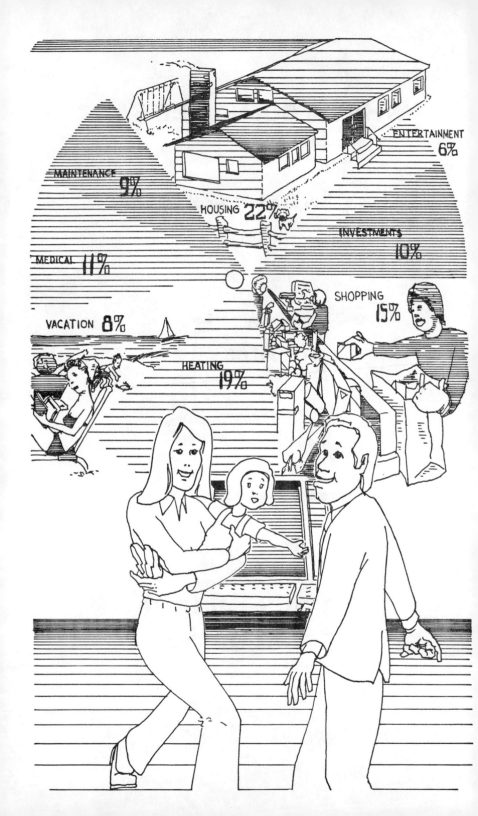

FAMILY BUDGET MANAGEMENT

Any well run business runs on budgets—that's an established fact. From ma and pa stores to giant corporations, budgeting is, or should be, a way of life.

There's no reason a family can't operate the same way. Many do, and with the aid of software developed for this purpose, budgeting now is easy and can potentially save you hundreds or even thousands of dollars.

Here again, these programs generally ask you for all kinds of data for the variables at hand: salary of one or more family members, housing expenses, food costs, etc. You can plug in these numbers from prior years when you didn't budget to see how you would have done.

Or you can take realistic estimates for the upcoming year and enter those figures. The programs can take this information and compute the various percentages of the gross income that each item takes. As a rule of thumb, housing should be no more than ¼ of your gross income. After your numbers have been put in, the computer can adjust for taxes and flag warning areas.

If you're using this tool to see whether or not you can afford a new house, you'll have the answer. If it's to keep track of household expenses in order to keep them in line, no problem either. And if you use it to analyze your tax situation by using those numbers in the FAMILY BUDGET MANAGEMEMT programs commercially available, you'll get still additional information which can help you make better decisions.

With prices that always increase, year after year, all families except the super wealthy should be on budgets. At the very least you'll know what you spent and where you spent it. At the other end of the pole, you can save money and frustration by sticking to a well planned budget...created with the help, of course, of your personal computer.

WHAT A COMPUTER CAN DO FOR YOU

Home Uses For A Personal Computer

Area
6

Controlling

CONTROLLING

In addition to the many database type uses presented in this book, there is another class of programs which is extremely useful to homeowners.

CONTROLLING programs running on your personal computer enable you to:

- set up a burglar alarm system
- monitor your heating and cooling
- compute energy usage and savings
- operate appliances in the home
- keep time in many different ways

In addition to the operation of devices in the home, these programs can actually save you money, in several ways.

First, having your personal computer control devices can eliminate the purchase of the devices separately (i.e. burglar alarm). You will, of course, have to purchase hardware and software, but the total cost is likely to be less or at least competitive.

Secondly, and perhaps the most important reason, is that these programs, expecially in the area of energy usage, can compute your requirments, usage and areas of heat/cold loss. The result when these factors are combined could be a reduction in your energy bills if recommended procedures are chosen.

People tend naturally to be wasteful when it comes to energy, and now there's a perfect opportunity for the alleviation of this waste. All it requires is an initial purchase and set-up and then the computer does it all for you.

It's yet another practical, useful area that shouldn't be overlooked, whether you own a micro computer or are thinking about buying one.

WHAT A COMPUTER CAN DO FOR YOU

Home Uses For A Personal Computer

Area
7

Health And Diet Management

HEALTH AND DIET MANAGEMENT

Among the many highly personal uses for a micro computer are the food and body related programs available.

While at first it may seem trivial to have your computer keep track of recipes, a second look will show some pretty good and important uses for the same database.

Let's assume you purchase one of the commercial programs which stores your recipes, allowing you room for ingredients, costs, amounts, procedures and so forth. Not only can you call up any recipe at any time, you can also:

• Create a shopping list, which automatically combines like ingredients for one or more weeks at a time! If you use sugar in 7 different recipies in varying amounts, the computer will add it all up and let you know how much you need in total. This usually leads to savings from not overbuying.

• Suppose you are planning a party for 24 people. You can call up the recipe, and have the computer figure out the quantities needed to serve 24, and create the usual shopping list for the same.

• If you are in business baking or catering as a sideline or full time profession, as many are, your costs on any recipe for any number of people can be quickly computed.

This is just the area of recipe management for daily living. Take the same data and information, and you can extract diet information, like how high or low your protien or cholesterol intake is with a certain menu over a 1 - 2 week period. In fact, some programs even will print out suggested meal plans depending on your dieting and vitamin requirements.

Once again, it's all a matter of taking a database (recipes, foods, etc.), organizing it, and manipulating it to get information which can help you.

The final programs available in the area of HEALTH & DIET MANAGEMENT includes exercise software. Here you can put in such vital information as height, weight, age, health items and a recommended exercise program.

Of course, the computer is never meant to replace the doctor, but for many people, some common sense and a personal computer can point you in the right direction. Many of these health programs have been written by or in conjunction with nutritionists and doctors.

While you shouldn't purchase a computer solely for these benefits, they are avenues of use that many people who own computers don't take advantage of. Remember, your computer is insatiable for the amount of work it can do...don't overlook any area that could benefit you.

WHAT A COMPUTER CAN DO FOR YOU

Home Uses For A Personal Computer

Collectibles Management

COLLECTIBLES MANAGEMENT

Most everyone collects something, whether it be stamps, coins, antiques, model cars, magazines, records, or books.

It seems rather obvious that if you collect antique cars, you don't need to catalogue them, since you'd probably only own a couple.

But what about a stamp collection, with perhaps hundreds or even thousands of items in it? Or baseball cards, where every year has a new set?

As you probably can guess, the personal computer's database management system is ideal for managing collections of any kind. Let's look at what you'd want to do.

In addition to having a separate record for each item, you'd also want to be able to add up either the total cost or value of the collection. You might also want to search out items in a certain year, condition, or category—1956 baseball cards, stamps about John F. Kennedy or antiques in mint condition.

Here's how a field set-up for a stamp collection might look. You can add or modify fields for your own collection.

1 CATALOG NUMBER
2 NAME OR IDENTIFYING TITLE
3 SUBJECT
4 YEAR (OR DATE) ISSUED
5 CONDITION
6 YOUR COST
7 CURRENT VALUE
8 COLOR
9 SIZE
10 COUNTRY
11 QUALITY
12 COMMENTS
13 MISCELLANEOUS

With a DBMS system, you can now add up the totals in fields #6 and #7 to find what you paid for the collection and what it's now worth. You can print out, for example, only those stamps of a given country, or stamps with certain catalog numbers. You have total flexibility with any kind of collection, and managing it on your personal computer leaves time for the real fun of collecting— enjoying your collection for beauty and/or investment.

WHAT A COMPUTER CAN DO FOR YOU

Home Uses For A Personal Computer

Area
9

Word Processing

WORD PROCESSING

Of all the buzzwords of the computer industry, word processing is probably the most well known amongst non-computer people. The phrase 'word processing' is well chosen, for the area it covers goes beyond writing letters and other documents.

Words, like numbers, can be processed, manipulated and managed by a computer system. Word processing refers primarily to the management of documents containing words to make their production and transmission faster and more efficient.

For example, this book was written on a personal computer using a word processing program. Instead of typing the manuscript on paper, I typed it into the computer, where it was stored. At any time, I could edit, change or add new sentences anywhere in the book, and all this editing was done on the screen, thus eliminating the need for retyping on paper.

When this book, or your letters or other documents are correct, you assign various codes determining the width of the letter, the length of the page, whether or not to center or have flush margins, and just press a button and the printer or typewriter will reproduce the letter, perfectly. You can then edit your letter and print it out again, without having to waste time and labor in retyping the whole letter.

A major benefit of having all your correspondence on computer is storage. Instead of filing away letters in a file drawer, you could view any letter by simply calling it up on the screen. This is one step in the overall move to eliminate the extraordinary paper waste that both businesses and people seem to have.

To this point, word processing enables us to create documents, edit them and print them out in any format, depending on your purpose. It also gives us the opportunity to store our correspondence for future viewing and editing. But there's more.

In an offshoot of this area which will be more fully discussed in Chapter 19, you can send your document over the phone lines to anyone having a personal computer and the ability to receive your words. This letter could appear on that person's screen or be printed at that location. This word processing/communications technique is primarily used in business, but the time for personal use is just around the corner.

Word processing programs, for the most part, are menu driven (you are given a choice of what you want to do) and easy to operate.

The typical choices you have are as follows:

1 CLEAR THE FILE (MEMORY) OF ANY PREVIOUS LETTERS
2 TYPE IN A LETTER
3 SAVE A LETTER
4 REVISE A LETTER
5 SET UP A PRINTER CONFIGURATION (WIDTHS, LENGTH, MARGINS, ETC)
6 COMBINE TWO OR MORE LETTERS
7 CALL UP ANOTHER LETTER
8 PROTECT A LETTER
9 PRINT OUT THE LETTER

I have used the term letter for simplicity, but whether it's a one page note or a book, the use, operation, and purpose of word processing is still the same: to save time, money, and labor by efficiently handling the printed word.

WHAT A COMPUTER CAN DO FOR YOU

Home Uses For A Personal Computer

Area
10

Insurance
Management

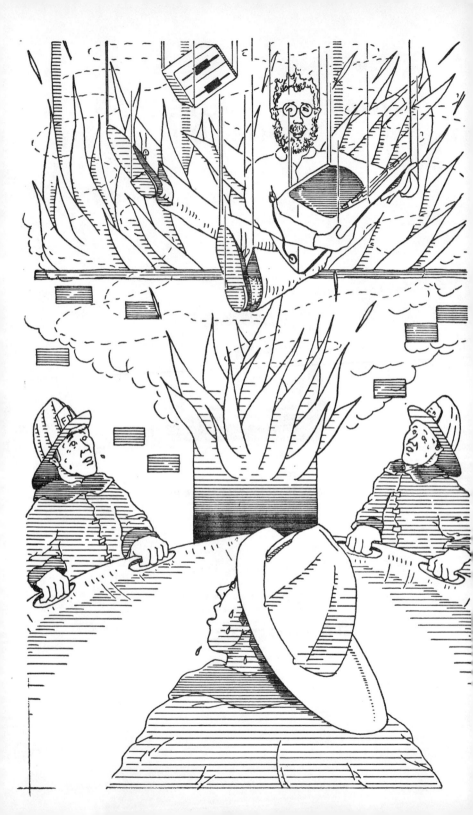

INSURANCE MANAGEMENT

We all pay our insurance premiums, but very few people take the time and effort to catalog their possessions. In the event of a fire, flood or other damaging event, the better the documentation of your possessions, the better the chance of collection.

Once again, the DBMS comes to the rescue. I have set up a very simple program on a DBMS basis, which lets me keep track of all my household possessions. I use one diskette per year, and enter whatever I have purchased in the last month.

Only 4 fields are necessary:

1 DATE
2 STORE
3 ITEM
4 PRICE

You simply enter in this information from your sales receipts or checkbook, and then alphabetize by type of item or date, whichever you prefer. At the end of a year, make a printout and a backup diskette. Store the printout and the backup in a safe or other fireproof place. Should you need this information, you have excellent proof of what you've owned. It's a lot of work to put in the items you already own, but in the event of a major disaster, it could mean a difference of $10,000 or $20,000, or maybe even more!

Other areas involving insurance are also benefitted by the personal computer. You can compare various policies, plugging in your vital information and seeing which coverage is best for you at the lowest cost.

Insurance, as it is such an intangible service, should, at the very least, be represented by something on paper letting you know what you own and what it's worth. Most people would tend to underestimate the value of the contents of their home; even with "padding" they'd probably still be under. All the $10 and $20 items really add up!

WHAT A COMPUTER CAN DO FOR YOU

Home Uses For A Personal Computer

Area
11

Income Tax Management

INCOME TAX MANAGEMENT

No single event is as important to Americans as taxes. Everyone, regardless how much they earn, has a keen interest in paying as little tax as possible, most everyone legally.

With the advent of the microcomputer, you can now prepare your taxes with ease, but more importantly, analyze different ways of preparing tax returns.

Basically, you can purchase ready made programs which ask you for the basic information—income, expenses, deductions, etc. But then, instead of just cranking out a return as you would, you get options.

A typical tax preparation program 'menu' might offer the following choices:

1 MARRIED COUPLE FILING JOINTLY AND ITEMIZING DEDUCTIONS
2 MARRIED COUPLE FILING SEPARATELY AND ITEMIZING DEDUCTIONS
3 MARRIED COUPLE FILING JOINTLY WITH STANDARD DEDUCTION
4 MARRIED COUPLE FILING SEPARATELY WITH STANDARD DEDUCTION

Some programs may be set up differently, asking you for the information in another way:

MARITAL STATUS

1 SINGLE
2 MARRIED

DEPENDENTS

1 0
2 1
3 2
4 3
5 4
6 ENTER NUMBER:

FILING STATUS

1 SEPARATELY
2 JOINTLY

DEDUCTIONS
1 ITEMIZE
2 STANDARD

As you can see, there are dozens of different combinations, which the computer can try for you. The result is simple: with the same initial information, you can compute your taxes in many different ways, leading you to the best possible route.

Of course, the listings above are simple, and most good tax programs have many more enhancements. But their basic premise is the same—the ability to try out different methods of computation quickly and efficiently.

Additionally, many of the tax programs can actually print out forms acceptable for returns by the IRS. Finally, you can store data from past years, so that you have all your records in one place—on a floppy disk! Remember, of course, to make a backup!!!

WHAT A COMPUTER CAN DO FOR YOU

Home Uses For A Personal Computer

Area
12

Investment
Management

INVESTMENT MANAGEMENT

Whether you have small amounts of monies in your bank and in the stock market or you are a major investor, the personal computer can help you in managing your investments.

There are four areas in which readily available programs can assist you. The first is computing return on various investments, so that you can compare alternatives. For example, you might be asked for the following information for any given investment:

1 AMOUNT TO BE INVESTED
2 LENGTH OF INVESTMENT
3 ANNUAL INTEREST RATE
4 DISCOUNT RATE IF ANY
5 CURRENT SELLING PRICE OF STOCK
6 NUMBER OF SHARES OR UNITS

All you really have to do is plug in the numbers in each case to determine which investment is the better. Of course, the computer can't predict the ups and downs of the various financial markets or interest rates, so in cases where the value of an investment fluctuates, you can only get an idea using the information you start with.

The second area is keeping track or monitoring your portfolio. You can, for each different financial instrument you own, insert the buy date, cost, and other information. By inserting current rates and prices, you can update your entire portfolio in seconds, and print it out on paper if you have a printer.

You'll also be able to see how much you made (or lost) and the current value of your investment, either by individual item or in total.

Another area is the analysis of stocks and other financial investments. You can, once again, insert numbers, ratios, and other financial information to get a comparison. Keep in mind that the computer is only tabulating and comparing information; it does not make recommendations.

The fourth and final area is the retrieval of stock market information direct from the markets themselves. Here's how it works.

Via a modem, or telephone linkup, and utilizing the correct software, you can hook up your personal computer to a major financial reporting source, and get up to date stock market quotes.

This would aid everyone from the person who wants to see how his stocks are doing, to the sophisticated investor who needs up to the minute information.

Through the phone linkup, you can also get other financial information, such as news stories, for your perusal. You can view them on the screen or have printouts made.

This area is wide open with many more new ways of utilizing the computer sure to come.

WHAT A COMPUTER CAN DO FOR YOU

Home Uses For A Personal Computer

Area
13

Home Buying

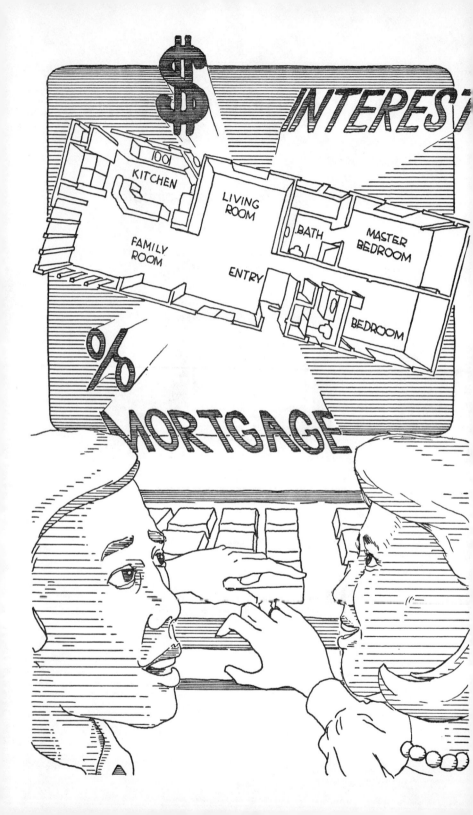

HOME BUYING

Half the trick in purchasing a new home is easy: finding the size, shape and features you want. Deciding on the layout and other visible features is really the fun in buying.

If you're like most people, then you dislike the other half: the financial matters, not only paying for the house, but wading through the many financial options open to a homebuyer.

You can use your personal computer to determine mortgage payments, based on the interest rate available to you, the length of time of the mortgage, and the amount. With the continual variation in interest rates as of late, knowing what you'd be paying at any given interest rate is important. The difference of a half or one percent can mean plenty of dollars per month.

Additionally, you can, with your computer, figure out the portion of your family's income a household will require. This can give you a good picture as to your capability to afford a given home.

You can also do a 'what if' analysis...that is, what if interest rates go down 2 percentage points by next year...does it pay to wait or buy? Or what if taxes and gas/electric go up by a certain figure...what does that do to the total picture.

Before you get into a house, it's always been a good idea to know all the financial ramifications. Now, with your microcomputer, it's much easier!

WHAT A COMPUTER CAN DO FOR YOU

Home Uses For A Personal Computer

**Area
14**

Medical Records
Management

MEDICAL RECORDS MANAGEMENT

Medical records are one of those items that families never get around to maintaining. But they are so important when an illness occurs.

Using a very simple data base program, you can construct a system to keep track of all of a family member's illnesses, allergies, treatments and medications.

Actually, you'll probably want to set up one file for each member of the family, and the fields you'd include might look like this:

1 NAME
2 CURRENT ADDRESS
3 SPOUSE
4 NEAREST RELATIVE
5 SEX
6 BLOOD TYPE
7 ALLERGIES
8 ALLERGIC TO MEDICATIONS?
9 HEIGHT
10 WEIGHT
11 EYES
12 MEDICAL VISITS - LIST EACH
13 LAST CHECKUP/PHYSICAL
14 INSURANCE CARRIERS & POLICY NUMBERS
15 EMPLOYER/ADDRESS/GROUP NUMBER

There is probably more information you'll want to include, but having this information handy is quite important.

It's also quite useful for insurance purposes, so that completing the forms takes less time when you have all the information. This is the reason for items 14 and 15.

It would also be a very good idea to make a printout for each member of the family and keep it in a central location that everyone in the family knows. You might want to keep an additional copy in a safe place, along with a backup copy of the diskette.

It shouldn't take that much time to set up this kind of file, and the value it has in an emergency will be worth many more times the initial energy expended.

WHAT A COMPUTER CAN DO FOR YOU

Home Uses For A Personal Computer

Area
15

Automobile Management & Trip Planning

AUTOMOBILE MANAGEMENT/TRIP PLANNING

Here's an interesting use for your micro computer. Most people don't keep written records for the necessary routine maintenance on their car, with the possible exception of oil changes and lubrications.

There are so many other aspects of your car's maintenance that only seem to be taken care of when something goes wrong. Many of these problems can be avoided by regular checks and maintenance, and keeping track of these items is simple for a basic data base management program, our old reliable.

You might set up a program that looks like this:

1 GREASE, OIL & FILTER (00000 MILES)
2 ROTATE TIRES (00000 TIRES)
3 CHECK HOSES AND VALVES (00000 MILES)
4 WINTERIZING (SEPTEMBER/OCTOBER)
5 CHECK SHOCK ABSORBERS (00000 MILES)
6 CHECK ALIGNMENT AND FRAME (00000 MILES)
7 CHECK ELECTRICAL SYSTEM (00000 MILES)
8 CHECK WATER LEVEL/WASHER FLUID (00000 MILES)

Each item, in addition to the number of miles you want to check it, would have room for the date last checked, and what was done. In this chart fashion, you could see at a glance what needs to be done by simply looking at the current mileage on your car.

Another usage, and there are currently programs available, is trip planning. You can actually plug into a computer your destination points and get an idea of the best way to go.

With a telephone linkup, you can gain access to information banks and get schedules of airplanes and trains for trip planning.

While the idea of maintaining your car's records may seem, at first, a bit too much, it has saved me plenty of money, by preventing breakdowns and other problems.

WHAT A COMPUTER CAN DO FOR YOU

Home Uses For A Personal Computer

Time Management

TIME MANAGEMENT

Once again we resort to our old standby, the data base management program, to help us in the management of time.

Most of us would get a lot more work (or study) done if we were better organized, and part of that organization can be handled on your personal computer.

As you get older, own a house, have a family, perhaps own a business, the amount of things you have to do at certain times of the year really add up.

The solution is quite easy. With a typical DBMS program, you set up one file for each month. In the file you list everything that you have to do that month. At first, this will seem unnecessary, but if you look at the wide diversity of items on this list, you'll see the importance of this idea.

1 INSPECT CARS
2 TURN ON/OFF HEAT
3 PLANT GRASS SEED
4 FILE INCOME TAX RETURNS
5 ARRANGE FOR ANNUAL SALES MEETING
6 TURN IN ENGLISH REPORT
7 START COOKING FOR SUMMER PARTY
8 PUT SNOW TIRES ON CAR
9 RESERVE PERMANENT TENNIS COURT TIME
10 FILE FOR HOMESTEAD REBATE
11 FILE SALES TAX RETURNS
12 SET UP YEARLY DOCTOR'S CHECKUP
13 REGISTER FOR FALL COURSE
14 ATTEND STAMP COLLECTORS SHOW
15 BUY AIR CONDITIONER
16 RENEW CERTIFICATE OF DEPOSIT
17 SEND OUT PARTY INVITATIONS
18 CHECK STOCK QUOTATIONS
19 SEND DEPOSIT FOR SUMMER RENTAL
20 MAIL BIRTHDAY CARD

This list could be a mile long, but if you place each item in the correct month, the whole concept suddenly makes a lot of sense.

You'd be able to call up all the things you have to do in any given month and get a printout of the same. It would be a checklist to make sure you don't overlook important dates.

There are programs out that handle short term time management, your daily appointments. You simply can program in everything that has to be done on a daily basis, along with times, and you're reminded appropriately.

As with every other idea in this book, choose those that are most important to you. But I think you'll agree that keeping track of time is one very important area.

WHAT A COMPUTER CAN DO FOR YOU

Business Uses For A Personal Computer

Area
17

Financial Analysis

FINANCIAL ANALYSIS

Every business, whether the corner deli or a giant corporation, needs some sort of financial analysis. If there's a small business in your future (or if you run one today) then you know about things like cash flow, return on investment, and so forth.

For most businesses, obviously, the degree of sophistication of financial analysis does not need to match that of large companies. But the need is still there, and many menu driven (giving you the choice) programs are available for the following areas of importance to a small business:

(1) BREAKEVEN POINT: every business must have a breakeven point, the point at which you start earning overall profits on the sale of goods or services. However, there are factors, such as fixed costs, that go into breakeven analysis that many people may simply overlook. Simple breakeven programs will ask for information like cost of goods sold, selling price, etc., and then determine breakeven in terms of dollars and units.

(2) CASH FLOW: this all important item in a small business' well being can be found in many business packages. It helps you determine your cash needs over a period of time, so that you don't run into situations where you can't meet your bills. Most stores borrow at certain times when cash flow is low, and also have a cash surplus when business is good. Cash flow analysis helps you smooth out the cash situation over the course of a year.

(3) FORECASTING: It's easy to say ''I think we'll do 10 percent more business next year'' but many businesses are finding that with the use of the computer, forecasting sales and profits can be more sophisticated than guessing. The more accurate your forecast, the better you can deal with purchasing, cash flow and other related items.

(4) INCOME/EXPENSE: when a business is in full swing, it's sometimes hard to tell, until the end of the year, if you're spending too much or too little in critical areas. If you have the luxury of an accountant coming in every month, you can get that information. But now your personal computer can also take your current expenses and income, compare them with years past, and show you any areas that vary from the norm. Then you can make adjustments as you see fit.

(5) DEPRECIATION: most people never understand how depreciation works...and for that reason perhaps don't take full advantage of its tax benefits. Most every business can benefit from utilizing depreciation of its assets, and easy to find computer programs make this now an easy job.

(6) RETURN ON INVESTMENT: it's one thing to be in business, another to make money, and a third to have a good return on investment. Determining your ROI (return on investment) will give you insight into the amount of time and energy you invest in a business and the financial rewards you get out of it. It might give you some interesting ideas on making your small business grow large.

(7) JOB PRICING/BIDDING: for many small businesses, getting jobs depends on the bids they submit. If you're a builder, for example, the time you expend analyzing jobs and preparing bids may be too high, expecially if you get many requests. You might find yourself spending all your time bidding and too little time building. The key to this dilemma are programs available to help you estimate job costs and prepare bids. It takes probably 1/5th to 1/10th the time as when done by hand.

Those are just a few of the many financial analysis programs available. Other areas covered include amortization, the various financial ratios, investment analysis and mortgage payments. There are software packages that offer all of the above and many more on one diskette, so you don't really need to buy a separate program for each task.

WHAT A COMPUTER CAN DO FOR YOU

Business Uses For A Personal Computer

Area
18

Word Processing

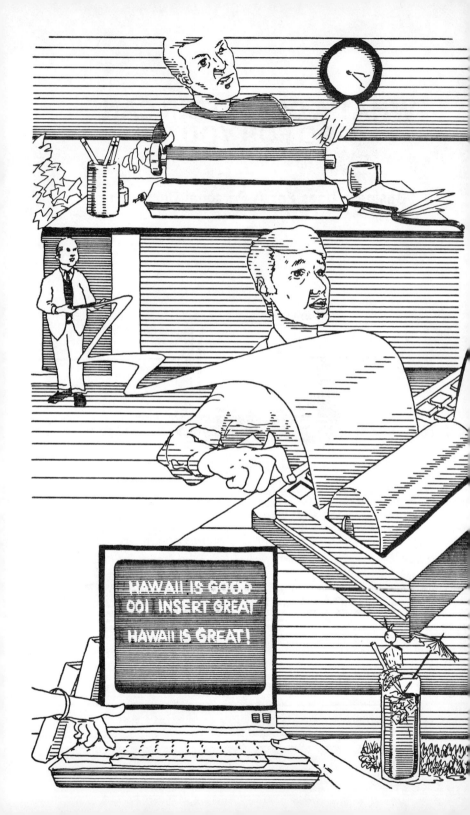

WORD PROCESSING

"Will someone tell me exactly what word processing is?" That's a question that so many people ask, so lets define it.

When you process anything, you perform certain operations, procedures, tasks or functions on the item you're processing. When the post office processes letters, it means postmarking and delivering. When teachers process report cards, it means making up the grades.

When small businesses, authors and individuals process words, it means they make the creation of documents, from one page letters to 500 page books, an easy task. Here's how they do it.

Assuming a personal computer is hooked up to a printer of some kind...for our discussion it doesn't matter which kind. The only requirement for a word processing system is a computer, a printer and the proper software.

Take the case of this series of books, which were written on a computer and handled with a popular word processing program.

After setting up your parameters (width and length of page, spacing, line skipping, indenting, etc.) you simply type your copy or words onto the computer keyboard. After you've typed in your letter, chapter or report, you save the material under a name you make up. In this case, I saved material area by area.

So now you have a mass of words inside the computer, ready for processing. The first stage is editing. You recall the information back up on the screen, and make changes right there. You don't have to type out the copy, erase, retype words like you used to do on paper. You can change the order of sentences, words, paragraphs or even whole sections.

You edit on the screen, avoiding time consuming typing and retyping. Now, for the final step in word processing: printing. You simply turn on your printer and walk away. The whole letter or document will be printed to your specifications, letter perfect.

If you come back and decide the width should be changed, as in the case of a book like this, you change one number, and then the document will be printed in a different width. The choices are yours, and what word processing eliminates is all the intermediate typing and retyping.

There are even enhancements now available where the computer can check all your spelling against a dictionary which comes on a diskette. Writing never used to be so easy. Now you spend less time on the mechanics and more on the writing!

But that's only the beginning of word processing's capabilities. With communications capabilities (see next section) you can send your letter or book over the phone lines across the country. You can also create camera-ready (clean, clear copy for a printer) copy for quick printing; this is excellent for reports you wish to make several copies of.

So when people ask you what word processing is, you'll be able to tell about a fascinating area, one made possible by the personal microcomputer.

WHAT A COMPUTER CAN DO FOR YOU

Business Uses For A Personal Computer

Communications

COMMUNICATIONS

One of the most dramatic uses for your personal computer will be communications—the transfer of information between two companies or individuals or any combination.

For businesses of any size, but especially for small firms, valuable time and efficiency will be gained by instant communication by computer, the ability to tap huge data banks with ease and already, you can belong to information networks such as The Source and CompuServe, which have everything from airline schedules to news reports to free classified advertising available. After joining, you simply dial their phone number through your computer phone hookup, called a modem, punch in your identification number and password, and you now have instant access to literally hundreds of subjects and possibilities.

These information networks, as they are called, are only one small part of the total picture. People already have a computer in the office, and a terminal at home. Feel like getting up late, working in your pajamas and not going into the office one day? Before personal computers, that would be impossible. Today it isn't—you can still do some work at home, as the information you enter is transmitted directly to the computer in your office.

What a great way of working for parents with young children at home, people in isolated, out-of-the-way locations and for days on which weather makes it impossible to get into work.

This space age technology, using already existing telephone lines, your personal computer, some additional hardware and software, has more communications benefits and uses.

Suppose you have two offices, one in New York and another in Los Angeles. Instead of phone calls and time consuming letters, you can now send letters, documents and even lengthy reports over the modem hookup, and have the document stored in the computer at your other office, and a paper copy printed out for whomever you wish.

This technology doesn't require huge computers with large staffs to maintain them. Today's microcomputers are capable of every communications usage mentioned here, plus every other use in this book.

But this is only the beginning. Imaginative business people will find more ways in which to use the communications capabilities of the personal computer. From a hobbyist point of view, you can "chat"—talk with other microcomputer owners—through your keyboard and modem. You can dial up bulletin boards—freelance, amateur message centers. You'll learn what people are doing around the country—and the world—and then perhaps utilize what you've learned in your business, or personal, situation.

In short, communications has been totally revolutionized by the computer, and taking advantage of these easy to use procedures will help every business, regardless of size, product or location.

WHAT A COMPUTER CAN DO FOR YOU

Business Uses For A Personal Computer

Area
20

Mailing List
Management

MAILING LIST MANAGEMENT

One of the most important assets of a small business is its mailing list. Customers that have already purchased something from you, whether it be a pair of pants or an oil change, represent people who probably were satisfied with your service and/or product, and who would probably buy from you again.

Therefore, the prudent use and maintenance of your up-to-date mailing list could be a major contributor to your business success. Smart business owners understand this, and take pains to keep their mailing lists clean.

As you can probably guess, maintaining a mailing list is as easy as DBMS—our old standby. Quite simply, you need to be able to compile names into a list which makes sense, and then alphabetize by customer name or zip code, for bulk mailings. There are plenty of stock programs that will handle this, but what this section concerns itself about more is creative uses for a mailing list.

With the costs of postage, printing and mailing always on the rise, the importance of targeting your mailings becomes very critical. Suppose you own a retail store with 5000 customers. You sell men's and women's fashions. If your list is coded properly, you should be able to do different mailings around these examples:

(1) a mailing to all women to announce a special sale on dresses;
(2) a mailing to all men to announce a sale on suits;
(3) a mailing to women who like a certain name brand of clothing to announce that their new fall line is in;
(4) a mailing to men on the same order;
(5) a mailing to residents of a certain town with a special promotion;
(6) a mailing to those people on your list who have a birthday in the next month;
(7) a mailing to those people on your list who have children, announcing a children's department.

And so forth. Once you set up your list with the right codes, you can sort and select out any portion of the list, thus being able to reach your prime prospects, those people most likely to respond to your offer.

One retailer friend of mine carries it one step further. His personal computer is hooked up to a typewriter. He types personal letters to selected customers for various promotions, using a carefully coded mailing list and a promotional approach to certain segments of the list at varying times.

Even if your business is small, maintaining and putting a mailing list to good use can't be overemphasized enough.

WHAT A COMPUTER CAN DO FOR YOU

Business Uses For A Personal Computer

Area
21

Customer File Management

CUSTOMER FILE MANAGEMENT

All businesses, of course, have customers. Whether it's a small town newspaper with lists of advertisers or a department store with 15,000 accounts, keeping track of customers in a meaningful manner is very important.

Using the data base management system as a framework, we can construct a customer file which can produce the type of information a business needs to function properly. Assume that for each customer, the following information is entered:

- name
- address
- city, state and zip
- phone
- family information
- profession
- credit limit
- current balance
- brand preference
- sales representative
- how long a customer
- homeowner/apartment dweller
- date of last order
- referrals

You may begin to see what good information about a businesses' customers means. Using the above information, a business manager can obtain each of these items for use indicated:

- a report of all customers with an outstanding balance over 30 days...for collection purposes.
- an index card file of customers sorted by sales rep's name...for sales call information.
- a list of all lawyers, for example...for a mailing about a new legal book.
- a list of brand preference...for research and promotion purposes for the advertising department.

• a list by people who haven't made a purchase in the last 60 days...for a "why haven't we seen you recently" followup campaign.

• a list of families with children...to see if a juvenile department warrants the investment.

A lot of these ideas sound a little like those presented in the mailing list area—they are. But here their use is for a different purpose—to gain statistical information about a firm's customers and provide people within the business with relevant information.

However, it is possible to combine the mailing list and customer files into one master list, providing you code everything properly. You will then have many powerful tools that many of your competitors won't—an accurate profile of your customer base, reports so your sales staff is working with accurate information and the ability to spend productive time on matters that count, not on meaningless tasks like searching a list of customers...one eagerly performed by your personal computer.

WHAT A COMPUTER CAN DO FOR YOU

Business Uses For A Personal Computer

Area
22

Inventory
Management

INVENTORY MANAGEMENT

Every business has an inventory—some you can see like oil drums, sneakers or bars of soap. Others, mainly the service businesses, have different kinds of inventories—such as advertising space, packages in transit or gallons of paint on hand. Whether you're a builder with a warehouse of supplies or a store with $1,000,000 worth of sporting goods, management of your inventory is very important.

You may think of your warehouse as old and dusty, but chances are you're paying anywhere from 10 to 20 percent to keep it full. So knowing what's in your inventory, it's current value and when you purchased it is critical.

There are general inventory programs available which, when customized or adapted to your own situation, can help you keep tabs on what you own. Other companies, if they structure a DBMS properly, can use a data base program as an inventory program.

The purpose of an inventory program is to give you instant information on what you purchased, what's been sold, and what remains. In this fashion, you can determine what products are selling well, and re-order those. You can also see which aren't moving and either place them on sale or cancel any outstanding orders. You can compare sales of certain items or brands between years or even months, to determine if there's a new trend there.

Your inventory management program has two major functions: to give you hard numbers used for accounting purposes; and to give you the ability to make decisions based on what is selling and what isn't.

Current programs give you the option to store and maintain the following information:

- vendor name
- address
- city/state/zip
- phone
- sales representative
- orders by date
- orders by style
- orders by size
- orders by color
- orders by completion date
  (date the goods are to be delivered)
- orders by brand
- orders by category or department

You can probably see that a well planned inventory program can yield valuable information. For example, suppose the local merchants decide to hold a sidewalk sale in the late spring. You can search your inventory and look for summer colors, a currently hot brand and those spring items that haven't been moving. In this fashion, you can make an intelligent decision, without wasting time, as to the items to put on sale.

This, of course, can all be done by hand. But imagine the hours it would take to count and categorize thousands of garments or hardware items.

But counting is only part of it. Breaking out your inventory by any type of category for various promotional purposes gives you an edge over competitors who just put on sale what they "think" they should. They're going by the seat of their pants; you're making smart decisions based on actual, up-to-date facts.

WHAT A COMPUTER CAN DO FOR YOU

Business Uses For A Personal Computer

Area
23

Accounting

ACCOUNTING

We all know how important keeping accurate records of income and expenses are—to satisfy the tax man when he cometh, but that is only one important use of the personal computer in the area of finances.

There are dozens of good accounting packages available for most brands of microcomputers. Depending on their price, some offer more than others. But in general, you should look for a package that handles all bookkeeping functions, general ledger work, accounts payable and receivable.

Other tasks that can be handled include payroll, government withholding forms, trial balance, income statement, balance sheet, journal entries and expense accounts.

If you're currently in business, then you are familiar with most of these jobs. If you're not, you will get to know them, in a most disdainful way as they represent nothing but paperwork. Necessary, but very time consuming, and unless you can afford the luxury of a paid bookkeeper, they're jobs you have to do yourself on a regular basis.

I am the perfect example of how a personal computer cut the time I spent on this type of work by 50 to 80 percent. Being a one man operation, my time is extremely valuable, split between seeing clients, designing ads, and paperwork.

I used to spend 5 hours per month just on my receivables and payables, putting little numbers in columns and adding them up. Now, it takes me no more than a half hour to enter the same information on my computer, and the addition, checking, placing numbers in columns, etc., is done automatically...and without errors as well. This frees up time for my other, more important tasks.

But as important as accurate records are, the major use for personal computers and accounting software is for the meaningful information produced, upon which business decisions are made.

An up-to-date set of figures will give you an accurate picture of profit and loss, and can be an important factor in your decision to increase or decrease inventory, advertising, sales force or other variables in your business. Having financial records at your fingertips gives you the ability to analyze your business and make forecasts and predictions.

One of the most popular programs in the financial area is a spreadsheet program. Here's how it works: you fill in all the information requested—sales, expenses, interest rates, amount borrowed, cost of goods, selling prices, and so forth. You then get an accurate picture of your projected profit and loss.

Then you now have the capability to ask "what if interest rates increase by 1 percent?" You simply enter the new interest rate, and the computer re-figures every single number dependent on the interest rate. In simple businesses, that could be 10 or 20 numbers. In a larger business, hundreds. In a second, you have the bottom line analysis to your "what/if" question. You can see that this type of analysis can give you valuable decision-making information.

The personal computer has made its mark in the financial arena, where it is used by one man to one thousand man companies, essentially for the same purposes. For the two major reasons—time savings and providing meaningful, decision-making information—it will continue as a mainstay in this area, yet another example of its versatility.

WHAT A COMPUTER CAN DO FOR YOU

Business Uses For A Personal Computer

Area
24

Production
Management

PRODUCTION MANAGEMENT

Any business that makes a product or some of those that supply certain services could probably find good uses from production management programs.

In any small service business, such as carpentry, plumbing, electrical, etc., or in small companies producing machined tools, parts and other products, it is important to be able to accurately figure the cost of a job.

Taking into account the cost of raw materials, labor to assemble or create the part, time involved, packaging, advertising, distribution costs, etc., your personal computer can help. In order to make a fair profit and stay in business, the estimation of a job's cost and finished price is most important.

Today's computer programs will ask you for all of the above information, and give you a breakeven analysis (how many you need to sell to break even) and a fixed/variable cost analysis. As good as a product is, it is very important to know this information—how much your investment is before one unit of your product is produced (fixed costs); how many you need to sell to meet your variable costs (costs that change directly with the number of units sold); and what an individual job costs in order to give out accurate price quotes.

Here again we use a form of the "what/if" program routine seen in previous areas. After plugging in all your information, you can now ask "What if I change the price of my widget from $1.32 to $1.22 and cut the competition's price? How much more business will I have to do if everything else stays the same?"

Like with the financial spreadsheets, as soon as the new price is entered, all numbers are recalculated and your new breakeven analysis is ready.

Another area in this realm of job pricing is bidding. Many types of jobs, from machinery to services, are won (and lost) by bidding. When you're preparing bids, that's time being used up for a job you may never get. You can now cut down on the time factor greatly, using the computer. Again, you simply enter the required information, and your bid is figured out automatically; you can even have it printed or typed direct from the computer so it is presentable. This is excellent where a firm makes many bids on a regular basis.

Some of these bidding programs are easy to write—you may not need to purchase a canned program, though they are available.

A final area within job pricing is price quoting. This is especially useful if your firm produces many different products, and your client calls up and asks " What is the price for 6 dozen widgets, 8 units of gadgets, 144 kidgets and a truckload of badgets?" Without having to call the customer back and waste 15 minutes, the computer has your answer in a second!

When shopping for programs in this area, make sure whichever you buy, or create yourself, can be modified to suit your business. While lumber is sold in running feet, electronic components may be sold by the gross. Therefore, you need to be able to customize the program to your own individual product or service, plus the way you have your business products categorized.

WHAT A COMPUTER CAN DO FOR YOU

Business Uses For A Personal Computer

Area
25

Loan Management

LOAN MANAGEMENT

Whether your current (or future) business has sales of $200,000 or $20 million, at some point you'll need to consider borrowing money for business purposes. You might need short term financing to cover anticipated receivables or long term debt for expansion. Whatever the case, you will have to know how to compare various alternatives of financial possibilities, with an eye towards getting the best value and lowest interest rates.

There are computer programs which take the information you feed it and analyze various financial instruments, such as loans, bonds and notes of various kinds. You can compare interest rates, length of loan and payment schedules to see exactly what you'll have to pay and when. In this fashion, you can make some very sensible decisions about borrowing money for your business.

You certainly do not have to be a financial wizard to analyze your options, just as you do not need to be a computer whiz to use today's personal computers. As we have seen throughout 'What a Computer Can Do For You', using a computer really is akin to answering questions and feeding in the information required. It's the same in this case.

You will be asked for the following information when computing the actual costs involved when borrowing:

AMOUNT OF PRINCIPAL: this is how much money you want to borrow.

INTEREST RATE: you simply plug in the interest rate being offered for each alternative.

TERM: here the computer is asking for the length of time of the loan—3 years, 20 years and so forth.

PAYMENT SCHEDULE: most are on a monthly basis, with some exceptions.

When you're finished, the computer will figure out your monthly payment, and give you a printout showing the principal and interest covered by each month's payment. Armed with a printout for each alternative course of action, you can then make the final decision on borrowing.

Of course, many businesses will never borrow money, but there is one consideration here. It is almost always better to borrow and work with other people's money to build a business than to keep sinking in your own funds. Realistically, not everyone applying for loans or credit lines will get them—but if you are considering a future business, you should know about financing and comparing alternatives.

WHAT A COMPUTER CAN DO FOR YOU

Education Uses For A Personal Computer

Area
26

Drill And Practice

EDUCATION: DRILL AND PRACTICE

I think it's safe to say we all have memories of learning addition and subtraction, memorizing dates of historical events and repeating the spelling of words until correct. For most people, this was a usually boring part of elementary education. In fact, many teachers have had problems in keeping students' attention when dealing with this type of subject matter.

This has been the case until now...until the computer entered the education area. Now children are suddenly much more interested, not because the subject matter has changed, but because the method of drill and practice has.

With an almost endless variety of choices in educational software, teaching and learning these once boring subjects is now interesting, colorful and in many cases exciting. Using the approach of instant feedback, students in all grades know instantly whether their answer is right or wrong. But let's start at the beginning.

Computer programs which handle drill and practice are set up as follows: the computer is programmed, usually by educators, with levels of difficulty. In simple addition, for example, the teacher can set the level of difficulty to single digit addition, double digits, or even triple or more. In this fashion, students learn how to add 2 + 5 before they learn 239 + 597. So, the computer is programmed with thousands of problems, in a logical sequence, and able to be started at any point.

A student starts at the beginning and receives the problem: 2 + 2. He must then press the correct answer. If he does, the computer presents another problem. If the student shows a mastery of this level by answering a set number of problems correctly, the computer program moves to the next level. In this case it might be still single digit numbers but with the totals requiring two digits: 5 + 8. After mastery of this level, the student would move on to the next level.

When a student gives a wrong answer, the computer responds with a gentle correction, which sometimes is humorous, so as to make the learning experience enjoyable and not painful. If a student has trouble at any level, the computer is programmed to stay on that level until the student has mastered it.

This system is applicable to spelling, history, science and most every educational area, from grade one to high school and beyond. There are even drill and practice style programs for high schoolers preparing for the SAT exams.

This type of program, of course, will not do away with the need for teachers, but more importantly free teachers up for closer work with individual students having special problems. Now students can work at their own pace, and from the early results, it seems as if the computer environment makes the once-thought-impossible task of teaching drill and practice a lot of fun!

The encouragement of the young person to use the computer at home with drill and practice is obvious. As with every subject in every school across the country, creating an atmosphere at home where the student wants to continue studying and working is a prime goal...on which often does not happen. The general consensus is that the computer can go a long way in giving the students a sense of interest in much of their schoolwork.

WHAT A COMPUTER CAN DO FOR YOU

Education Uses For A Personal Computer

Programming

EDUCATION: PROGRAMMING

Though I have deliberately not touched on programming in this book, now is the time for a brief introduction and the effect it has on educating our young people.

The computer is simply a machine. Like an automobile, bicycle or telephone, it needs instructions to function. A car needs someone to step on the gas to make it go forward; a bicycle needs someone to learn to make it turn. Similarly, a computer requires a set of instructions to make it do what you want it to.

Collectively, these instructions are called programs, or software. Creating them is called programming. Programming, contrary to what you might believe, is not reserved for university scholars and whiz kids. Today, programming personal computers is easy enough to understand by a large percentage of the population.

In fact, kids are learning to program their computers early on, and it is this quest for knowledge about making a computer work that is the subject of this section.

In order to illustrate how a grade school child would learn about programming, let's borrow the addition example from the last section. A child who has mastered the addition of three numbers may now ask "How can I make the computer add three numbers together?" It is this type of question which leads to programming.

At this point, a student would learn to write a program to add three numbers, which might look something like this:

```
10 PRINT "ENTER FIRST NUMBER";:INPUT A
20 PRINT "ENTER SECOND NUMBER";:INPUT B
30 PRINT "ENTER THIRD NUMBER";:INPUT C
40 SUM = A + B + C
50 PRINT "THE TOTAL IS "SUM
```

At first, this program may look a little complicated, but let's examine it. The first three lines (10,20,30) are instructing the student to tell the computer which three numbers to add. The next line says that the sum is equal to the addition of the three numbers, and the last line asks the computer to print out that total.

Now that a student has both mastered the addition of the three numbers and the writing of the program to add the same numbers, he already has learned more than the student who knows only how to add.

This may not seem like much in this elementary example, but when a student learns to program, he is learning much more than instructing a computer to add. One of the most lacking areas in students today is the ability to think logically; to draw conclusions based on fact and analysis rather than on emotions or guesswork.

In order to write programs, a student must develop his logical thinking abilities. Therefore, programming helps in the development of good thought processes in our youngsters. In my opinion, this is the most important area in which computers can help young people today. To be able to look at a problem, analyze it logically, and to construct a set of instructions to solve it is quite an accomplishment. If most every student learned simple programming at an early age, I think this country would have a significantly higher degree of literate and educated people, for most every decision we make in life stems from the ability to logically think something through.

So our second education area, that of programming, is extremely important. Once again, encouraging students at home to learn to program will undoubtedly have excellent results.

WHAT A COMPUTER CAN DO FOR YOU

Education Uses For A Personal Computer

Careers
And The Future

EDUCATION: CAREERS AND THE FUTURE

Much has been written about the use of computers in educating our young people, but an area which doesn't come up too often is the future course of our society and its effects on careers.

At this very moment, we are in the midst of a major transformation in our society. First, back in the 1800's, we were primarily an agricultural nation. Then, with the development of machines, we became an industrial nation. Many jobs were lost in the agricultural sector when automation and machines came along.

Now we are entering the third time period: the information age, which will bring with it similiar effects on the previous wave. Workers in our country will have to be retrained, and students will have to be educated towards handling information. The amount of employees in factories will decrease, while the numbers in businesses working with information will increase. It's an inevitable process.

Right now one of every two persons works with information— whether it be a computer company, a data processing firm, a research center or a publishing house. Assembly line workers—in the same fashion as agricultural workers—will have to prepare for and find other types of employment.

But what about students currently in school? This is the heart of this section—presenting the situation they face—and what to do about it.

Today's high school (or younger) student faces a work world vastly different than we knew when growing up. We're becoming a society of brains rather than muscle, and this means better education is necessary, smarter career planning critical and encouragement at all levels of maturation a must.

A student of today will grow up with computers, and chances are very good that any decent job in the future will require the basic knowledge of computer use or applications. No longer will it be good enough to be able bodied and have some degree of intelligence and basic training. Now, students will need to develop a sense of where they want to go, what their personal goals are and how they can best achieve them.

In fact, this area is so important, that I've written another book on the subject, "Getting Into Computers" which is due for publication by Ballentine Books in May, 1983. Students seriously interested in a career involving computing should look for this title when it is released.

In any event, this section's purpose is to make you aware of what will be happening in the future, in order that you can either better prepare for yourself, or assist someone else in planning for the future—a world where computers are as evident and important as the telephone is today.

WHAT A COMPUTER CAN DO FOR YOU

Entertainment With A Personal Computer

Area
29

Games

ENTERTAINMENT: GAMES

Probably the most outstanding feature of today's computer games is their imagination and cleverness. It's hard for most people to envision what chess or football would be like in a computer game. But in almost every case, these games prove to be challenging, enjoyable and better than expected.

If the only games you've seen or heard about are the outer space variety, you're in for a real surprise, for there are no less than 8 categories of games, each of which will be described briefly in this section.

SPACE GAMES

These are the action games that take place in outer space. Generally, you have the ability to shoot missiles to destroy invaders. But that's only the beginning. What these invaders can do (change shape, speed, direction or size) to make your job more difficult is what makes them so exciting. Whether you're the chaser or the chasee, the games get harder and harder as you get better.

STRATEGY/BATTLE GAMES

As a group, these games are thought provokers. It's you against the enemy in a real or imagined battle or other strategic situation. The game program gives the computer the ability to react to whatever moves you make. Therefore, every game is different in the same way all chess contests are different. With realistic figures and excellent graphics, it's easy to feel like you're on the battlefield.

BOARD GAMES

This group includes many of the oldest games invented by man: chess, checkers and backgammon. As you probably know, chess by computer has been brought to extensive heights as mainframe computers can compete on the master level. Even the personal computer versions are excellent, and as patient as can be.

CARD GAMES

The all night card game of the future could be you and your computer. Realistic programs are now available on which you can play or learn poker, bridge, gin and other popular card games. The computer can also, in some cases, play more than one hand...thus giving you a foursome!

FANTASY/ADVENTURE GAMES

You've probably heard about 'Dungeons and Dragons'...one of the hottest selling video games. Games like these have really caught on, as they involve living through a fantasy or exciting adventure. Generally, you are given a goal. To reach this goal, you must go through or overcome certain obstacles, all of which are designed to prevent your success. Every move you make results in the computer's reaction. Often times, it remembers better than you do!

PARTY GAMES

While there are light games for groups, this section of games has some you may not believe. Even pornography, mostly tastefully packaged and programmed, has managed not to be missed by computer buffs. As computers become the newest conversation item at parties, what better way than to let people get involved...with games that are respectfully raunchy and downright delirious!

SPORTS GAMES

This group has two parts: the action side, where you actually play against the computer; and the strategy games, where you call the plays, the computer then responding with stored information. Whether you like dribbling a ball down the basketball court or attempting to outsmart the opposing football coach, there's a sporting game for you and your micro computer.

GAMBLING GAMES

Some people take gambling seriously and to others its a once in a while proposition. You will find programs designed to help predict sporting events, especially horse races and football games. These programs take past data, and with a formula developed by the handicapper, compute the results with lightning speed. These programs are really just calculators that take factors deemed important, weigh them and find the totals. As with handicapping systems done by hand, their success rate is questionable. But, they ARE fun!

There you have it...games for every occasion, every taste and every desire. Once again, the ability to switch from a complicated game of bridge to a fast action space war shows the versatility of the computer. You'll come to appreciate being able, additionally, to turn off family budgeting or sales forecasts and sneak in a game of 'Space Invaders' or 'Backgammon' whenever you please. And the best part is...the computer will never tell!

WHAT A COMPUTER CAN DO FOR YOU

Entertainment With A Personal Computer

The Arts

ENTERTAINMENT: THE ARTS

This is probably the last area you'd expect to find in a computer book, but surprisingly to many, the field of computer art and music is one of the most exciting and fastest growing of all the applications areas!

When we think of fine art, names like Picasso and Van Gogh come to mind. When we think of great composers, Bach and Beethoven are easily remembered. But that may change in the future—great artists and composers may be people like you and me...in conjunction with their personal computer!

There are programs out on the market which enable you to write musical scores. You can change the beat, tempo and other musical variables and the computer rewrites the whole score! Even if you can't carry a tune, you can now write music, using programs which are surprisingly easy to understand.

The same is true with art: you can use special drawing boards to create new types of art. For example, you can draw a set of concentric circles; then you can instruct the computer to elongate one area, push another area up and yet another area down. What you can end up with is a three dimensional figure which can be changed over and over.

Much of the space age effects you see in movies such as Walt Disney's 'Tron' are produced by computers. This whole area is referred to as computer graphics and animation. It gives the user the ability to experiment with a wide variety of shapes without having to draw new ones each time. The computer can even store these shapes on your diskettes for future use.

To illustrate the popularity of this area, there are publications (The Computer Music Journal) and organizations; in New York there's even a gallery specializing in computer generated art!

So here's an 'entertainment' area you'd never expect...and one that can provide hours of endless fun and creative productions.

WHAT A COMPUTER CAN DO FOR YOU

Entertainment With A Personal Computer

Miscellaneous

ENTERTAINMENT: MISCELLANEOUS

When it comes to entertainment, playing games and creating paintings are only the beginning.

The personal computer makes most any hobby much more enjoyable. I collect stamps, and much of the time I used to spend was in cataloging the stamps I owned. Now, with the use of a data base program, cataloging my collection is quick and easy—leaving me more time to enjoy the collection I have.

This is true no matter what you collect—coins, dolls, beer cans, antiques. This is a prime example of how the computer can handle dull and routine tasks and give you more time to enjoy your hobby.

In setting up a data base program for any type of collection, you might use these basic fields plus any other special codes you need:

1. ITEM NAME
2. COUNTRY/STATE/CITY OF ORIGIN
3. DATE MINTED/ISSUED
4. CONDITION
5. ORIGINAL COST
6. DATE PURCHASED
7. CURRENT VALUE
8. CATALOG NUMBER
9. QUANTITY ISSUED

Use the data base program technique we have discussed often when creating a catalog for your collection. If you don't want to create your own, there are programs starting to appear that have been written especially to handle collections of various kinds. You'll have to search them out.

One additional area of entertainment is the computer itself. It is estimated that ⅔ of all computer owners spend time "just tinkering" and experimenting with their microcomputer.

Whether you're a dyed-in-the-wool hobbyist who builds his own computer components or a part time experimenter like I am, your computer itself can be a source of continuing entertainment and enjoyment.

When you own a computer, you'll discover that there's much you can find out that you won't find in the manual. You'll discover better ways to write programs, new uses for hardware and ways to increase the performance of your system. There is something inherently enjoyable about creating a program to do something unique—something you want it to do. That's the challenge. When it works, that's the reward.

So in conclusion, entertainment varies from the sheer joy of programming to space age games; from thought provoking mind activities to hobbies. The personal computer is easily used with all of these...plus any more you can create!

WHAT A COMPUTER CAN DO FOR YOU

Communicating With A Personal Computer

Computer Talk

COMPUTER TALK

Throughout this book we've seen the many applications computers have, in both business and personal situations. At this point, you should have several ideas of how you would make use of a computer. This section, as you'll see, opens up another entire new area, one which can work alone or with most every one of the ideas already presented.

Starting back in the early days of our country, the only way to communicate with people was through written letters delivered by The Pony Express, which took days, or weeks, to reach their destinations. Next came the automobile, which reduced the amount of time, and the telephone/telegraph, which enabled instant transmission of a message. But you had to speak the message, not give it in writing. The airplane made written messages even faster, and at this point, most written documents can be gotten to their destination overnight.

Which brings us to the next frontier in written communications delivery: electronic mail. Very simply, anyone with a personal computer, a telephone linkup (modem) and the proper software, can send messages to people or companies with computers, and have them receive a message instantly, viewing it both on the screen and having a printer create a hard copy.

You can "call" your friends, business associates or people at random and "chat" through your computer. You'll fire messages back and forth over the phone lines.

The personal computer not only works at home or business to manage the family budget or keep track of inventory, but as a communications tool enabling you to, literally, have access to the world!

In addition to calling people via your microcomputer, you can now access one of several major information services. These companies store huge amounts of data (stock market quotations, news, career information, sports, airline schedules, etc.) on large, mainframe computers. Upon becoming a member, you can dial up the service at any time and obtain only the information you desire. You pay only for the actual time you are connected to the main computer. This puts you in instant contact with a wealth of information, so whether you're researching a report or book or planning a vacation, you now have the access to instant information.

Another area of communications that links you with people who own computers similar to yours are bulletin boards. Again, with a modem and the proper software, you can call up any bulletin board around the country, either to find out information on a specific topic or just to chat about a programming problem you're having. People and groups run these bulletin boards, and listings of them are usually printed in some of the computer publications. It's another interesting form of communications, enabling you to meet people through your computer.

A final area of communications is a face-to-face one, which might seem out of place in light of what we've just seen. But computer clubs and user groups are springing up across the country at a fantastic pace. These groups get together on some sort of regular basis, in order to discuss needs and problems, and in some cases, form a cooperative for buying hardware and software. Computer clubs bring you in touch with people locally who share the same interest as you do—computing!

You also have the capability to send information which you've created over the phone lines, to help you in the home or at business. For example, suppose you've catalogued your stamp collection on a data base system. Assume you want to send a printout of all the stamps you own to a dealer for appraisal. You can either mail a printout or transmit the information over the phone line. This method is used a lot in business, especially between branch offices of a company. As we have already seen, it alleviates two things: the time spent in writing the information, and the dependency on the mails, two important factors in business, where time is money.

Communications might dwarf many of the other uses for personal computers, but in my opinion it's one area of many that can give you endless use and satisfaction.

Notes

Notes

Notes

Notes

We've got more great computer books coming your way!

We're busy developing more computer titles for you...and we'd love to put you on our mailing list to let you know when our books will be in your favorite stores. Kindly fill out this page and return to the address below.

Name _____

Address _____

City _____

State _____ Zip _____

1. Currently own a computer?   ( ) YES   ( ) NO

   If "Yes", which brand? _____

   _____

2. Planning to buy a computer?   ( ) YES   ( ) NO

3. Where did you buy this book? _____